I0755137
TUBMAN
Black American
Women Serving in the
WAVES and SARS WWII

ISBN: 978-1-953824-18-9

Printed in the United States of America

In the making of this book, every attempt has been made to verify names, facts, and figures.

Photos Public Domain

Cover design and book layout by Priscilla T Graham

Written by Priscilla T Graham
www.priscillatgraham.com

Dedicated to the Negro Women of WWII

WHAT PAY DOES A NAVY WAVE GET?

RATE	Monthly Base Pay—Clear	Food Allowance*	Quarters Allowance*	Total Income
Apprentice Seaman	$50.00	$54.00	$37.50	$141.50
Seaman Second Class	54.00	54.00	37.50	145.50
Seaman First Class	66.00	54.00	37.50	157.50
Petty Officer Third Class	78.00	54.00	37.50	169.50
Petty Officer Second Class	96.00	54.00	37.50	187.50
Petty Officer First Class	114.00	54.00	37.50	205.50
Chief Petty Officer Acting Appointment	126.00	54.00	37.50	217.50
Chief Petty Officer Permanent Appointment	138.00	54.00	37.50	229.50

*(Unless food and quarters are provided by Navy)

In addition, a WAVE receives $200 for clothing, the finest medical and dental care, special tax exemption, low-cost Government life insurance, and such privileges as free mail, reduced rates on transportation, theatre tickets, etc.

Your Navy needs you in the **WAVES**

ORDER NO. 72

Contents

Introduction

World War II was a defining moment in global history, and within its vast story lie countless individual narratives of bravery, sacrifice, and unshakable determination. Among these are the stories of the WAVES, SPARS, and the extraordinary Black Americans, service members, performers, activists, and leaders, whose contributions reshaped both the war effort and the nation's understanding of citizenship and equality.

This book brings these stories together. It highlights the women who broke barriers to serve in naval and coast guard units; the entertainers who risked their safety to uplift troops; the activists who challenged discriminatory practices; and the individuals honored with Liberty Ships bearing their names. Through photographs, historical records, and biographical sketches, this collection preserves the legacy of those who carved a path forward when opportunity was limited and recognition was scarce.

Their journeys, marked by courage, persistence, and unwavering patriotism, reveal a powerful truth: progress is built through the strength and vision of those willing to defy expectations. By revisiting their achievements, we honor the foundation they laid and ensure their contributions continue to inspire future generations.

This book invites readers to explore a vital, often overlooked chapter of American history, one defined by service, dignity, and the unrelenting pursuit of equality.

Captain Causey swearing in the first Negro WAVE at Indiana Headquarters

WAVES

The Women Accepted for Volunteer Emergency Service (WAVES) program was established by Congress and signed into law by President Franklin D. Roosevelt on July 21, 1942, creating the first women's branch of the U.S. Naval Reserve. The program was designed to fill critical wartime shortages by assigning women to shore-based administrative, communications, medical, and technical roles, thereby freeing more men for sea duty. Over the course of World War II, nearly 100,000 women served in the WAVES, stationed at more than 900 naval facilities across the United States.

Despite this groundbreaking expansion of women's service, the WAVES reflected the racial segregation of the era. For more than two years after its creation, Black women were barred from joining, even though Black men had served in the Navy since the 19th century and Black women were already serving in the Women's Army Corps and the Army Nurse Corps. The exclusion stemmed from long-standing Navy policies that restricted African Americans to limited roles and resisted integration more strongly than the Army.

Pressure for change intensified throughout 1943 and 1944. Civil rights organizations, Black newspapers, and women's advocacy groups publicly challenged the Navy's discriminatory stance. Inside the federal government, WAVES Director Mildred McAfee, the first woman commissioned as a naval officer, argued that the program could not claim national representation while excluding Black women. She found a powerful ally in Mary McLeod Bethune, educator, stateswoman, and founder of the National Council of Negro Women, who used her influence within the Roosevelt administration to push for full inclusion.

Their combined advocacy, along with the death of segregationist Navy Secretary Frank Knox, helped shift policy at the highest levels. On October 19, 1944, the Navy officially opened the WAVES to Black women. Ultimately, 72 Black women were accepted into the integrated Navy Reserve, marking the first time Black and white women trained and served together in the same naval program.

Among the most significant milestones was the commissioning of Harriet Ida Pickens and Frances Wills, who graduated from the Naval Reserve Midshipmen's School at Smith College on December 21, 1944. They became the first Black women officers in the WAVES and symbols of the program's long-delayed integration.

Although their numbers were small, the service of these 72 women had a lasting impact. Their presence challenged entrenched racial barriers within the Navy and contributed to the momentum that led to the desegregation of the U.S. military in 1948 under President Harry S. Truman. Their service also broadened the historical narrative of American women in uniform, ensuring that the contributions of Black women were recognized as part of the nation's wartime effort.

Frances Wills being sworn into the Navy on November 16, 1944, as Apprentice Seaman by Lieutenant Rosamond D. Selle, USNR, New York City.

Harriett Ida Pickens being sworn into the Navy on November 16, 1944, as an Apprentice Seaman by Lieutenant Rosamond D. Selle, USNR, New York City.

Frances Wills and Harriett Ida Pickens being sworn into the Navy on November 16, 1944, as Apprentice Seaman by Lieutenant Rosamond D. Selle, USNR, New York City. Willis, a Philadelphia native and adoption agent, and Pickens, a public health administrator, were the first Negro Naval Officers in the military to serve as WAVES, Women Accepted for Volunteer Emergency Service. They graduated from the Naval Reserve Midshipmen's School at Northampton, Massachusetts, in December 1944.

WAVES dressed up for the NAS Seattle, Spring Formal Dance. Left to right: Jeanne McIver, Harriet Berry, Muriel Alberti, Nancy Grant, Maleina Bagley, and Matti Ethridge. April 10, 1944

Lieutenant Pickens and Ensign Wills, Hunter Naval Training Station, New York trainers, photographed after graduation, visiting a shipyard in Brooklyn.

Lieutenant Harriett Ida Pickens and Ensign Frances Wills first Negro WAVES to be commissioned. They were members of the final graduating class at Naval Reserve Midshipmen's School at Northampton, Massachusetts on December 21, 1944

Naval Reserve Midshipmen's School at Northampton, Massachusetts on December 21, 1944 parade of members and officers of the school's final graduating class.

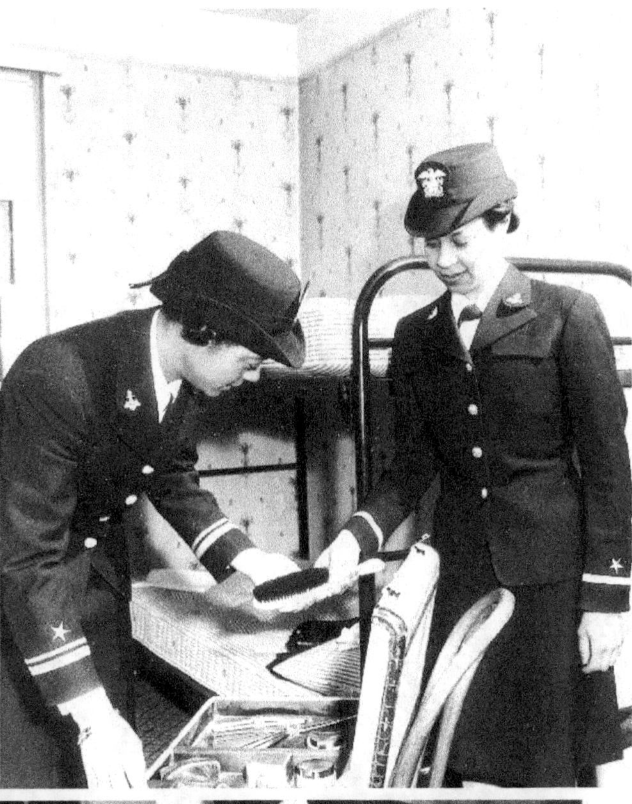

WAVES Apprentice Seaman Frances Bates, boot, inspecting a Grumman Wildcat engine on display at the US Naval Training School (WR) in Bronx, New York.

Commander Thomas A. Gaylord, USN, administers the oath on March 8, 1945, to five new Navy nurses commissioned in New York. Phyllis Mae Dailey, second from the right, was the first Negro woman sworn into the Navy. She was a nurse and a Columbia University student from New York. There were only four Negro women to serve in the Navy during World War II. On January 25, 1945, the Navy changed its policies to allow Negro women serve.

Hospital Apprentice School Second Class Ruth C. Isaacs, Katherine Horton, and Inez Patterson are the first Negro WAVES to enter the Hospital Corps School at National Naval Medical Center, Bethesda, Maryland, March 2, 1945

Hospital Apprentice School Second Class Ruth C. Isaacs, Katherine Horton, and Inez Patterson are the first Negro WAVES to enter the Hospital Corps School at National Naval Medical Center, Bethesda, Maryland March 2, 1945

Phyllis Mae Daley was the first Negro nurse to receive a commission in the Navy Corps. She is standing with other recruits beside a poster. March 8, 1945

Negro WAVES meeting with a group of visiting civilians at the Naval Operating Base in San Diego, California June 21, 1945

Olivia Hooker

Olivia Hooker was the first Negro woman to serve on active duty in the US Coast Guard in 1945. She was one of only five Negro women to first enlist in the SPAR program.

SPARS

The United States Coast Guard Women's Reserve, known as the SPARS, was established by Congress and signed into law by President Franklin D. Roosevelt on November 23, 1942, during the height of World War II. The legislation authorized the Coast Guard to accept women as both commissioned officers and enlisted personnel for the duration of the war plus six months, marking a historic expansion of women's military service. The name "SPARS" was derived from the Coast Guard motto *Semper Paratus*— "*Always Ready*"—and symbolized the readiness of American women to step into national defense roles.

The first SPARS were drawn from the Navy's WAVES program, reflecting the urgency of the wartime manpower crisis. As the Coast Guard's responsibilities grew, port security, convoy escort coordination, coastal patrols, intelligence gathering, and maritime communications, the service faced severe personnel shortages. The SPARS were created to release officers and enlisted men for sea duty, filling their positions at shore stations across the country. Women served in various roles, including communications, cryptography, clerical administration, supply, meteorology, radio operations, and training support, becoming an essential part of the Coast Guard's wartime infrastructure.

Training for enlisted SPARS took place at the Sheepshead Bay Maritime Training Station in New York, where women learned the fundamentals of seamanship, naval customs, military discipline, and the specialized skills required for their assignments. Officer candidates trained at the Coast Guard Academy in New London, Connecticut, making the SPARS the first women ever to receive formal instruction on the grounds of a federal service academy.

Despite the program's significance, the SPARS reflected the racial segregation policies of the era. Negro women were barred from joining until February 1945, more than two years after the program's creation and long after the WAVES had begun integrating. The Coast Guard, like the Navy, had a long history of restricting African Americans to limited roles, and the inclusion of Black women required sustained pressure from civil rights leaders, women's organizations, and federal advisors.

That barrier finally broke in early 1945. In March 1945, the first group of Negro women was accepted into the SPARS: Olivia Hooker, Dorothy Winifred Byrd, Julia Mosely, Yvonne Cumberbatch, and Aileen Cooke. Their enlistment marked a quiet but profound milestone. These women trained and served in a military branch that had never before admitted Black women, challenging long-standing racial barriers within the Coast Guard and expanding the meaning of wartime service.

Olivia Hooker, who later became a distinguished psychologist and professor, is often recognized as the first Black woman to wear the Coast Guard uniform. She and her fellow SPARS served in administrative and technical roles, proving their competence and professionalism in every assignment. Their presence helped lay the groundwork for the broader desegregation of the U.S. armed forces in 1948 under President Harry S. Truman.

Although the SPARS were demobilized after the war, their contributions reshaped the Coast Guard. They demonstrated that women could serve with discipline, technical skill, and leadership in every assignment they were given. The integration of Black women in 1945, though late and limited, remains one of the most significant civil rights milestones in Coast Guard history.
The legacy of the SPARS endures in every woman who serves in the Coast Guard today. Their wartime service, especially the pioneering steps taken by the first Black SPARS, stands as a testament to determination, patriotism, and the ongoing struggle for equality within America's military institutions.

SPAR recruits Julie Moseley Pole and Winifred Byrd

Prentice Seaman Anita Cook receiving her boot course at a US Training Station, Manhattan Beach, Brooklyn, New York

SPARs Apprentice Seaman Olivia Hooker and Aileen Anita Cook pause on the ladder of a dry-land ship USS Neversail during boot training at the US Coast Guard Basic Training Station, Manhattan Beach, Brooklyn, New York.

Josephine Baker

Josephine Baker, *Black Pearl, Bronze Venus, and the Creole Goddess,* was the first Negro to become a worldwide entertainer and star in a major motion picture, Marc Allégret. Baker renounced her US citizenship and became a French national after marrying French Industrialist Jean Lion. She refused to perform for segregated audiences even though a Miami Club offered her $10,000 to perform. The club later met her demands for mixed audiences. This helped integrate live entertainment shows in Las Vegas, Nevada.

During World War II, Josephine Baker, French Resistance Agent, was recruited by the Deuxieme Bureau, French Military as a spy. She collected information from officials about German troop locations during parties throughout her tour travels in Europe. Secret messages were written on sheet music with invisible ink. Baker would also sneak pictures of German military installations out of enemy territory by pinning them to her underwear and by placing other things in her luggage to smuggle in and out of the country.

Baker was promoted to Lieutenant in the Free French Air Force. She was awarded the Croix de guerre and Medal of Resistance by the French Military. Baker was named Chevalier of the Legion d'honneur by General Charles de Gaulle. *I have two loves my country and Paris.*

Baker is the only American to receive full French Military honors at her funeral. She died on April 12, 1975 from a cerebral hemorrhage.

Hattie McDaniel in uniform

Hattie McDaniel

Oscar Winner Hattie McDaniel, in front of her home on South Boulevard in Los Angeles, California, in 1942, led the Hollywood Victory Committee's Negro Division (AWVS). The performers traveled to military camps offering wartime entertainment to troops about to head overseas. McDaniel also helped entertain the soldiers and promoted the sale of war bonds.

Hattie McDaniel was the First Negro to win an Oscar in 1940 and the first Negro woman on radio, Hi Hat Hattie, KNX Radio Station, Los Angeles. When she attended the 12th Academy Awards at the Cocoanut Grove Night Club in the Ambassador Hotel, she had to sit at a small table in the back of the room because of the hotel's strict no Negroes policy. The producer of Gone with the Wind, David O. Selznick, convinced the hotel to make a special exception for Hattie McDaniel to attend.

In 1948, Hattie was instrumental in the US Supreme Court striking down restrictions against Negroes moving into the area.

Hattie McDaniel and General Benjamin Oliver Davis, Sr. the first Negro General in the United States Military

FIGHTING MEN VISIT WARNER BROS. STUDIO

Warner Brothers Studio

Hattie McDaniel, sepia screen star, takes out from her many civilians and war activities to escort three soldiers of a regiment stationed on the coast, around Warner Brothers Studio lot. Harry N. Warner, president of the company, broke a 30 year old rule when he autographed copies of the studio menu for Miss McDaniel's guests, Private Aaron Gaskins, Tech Sergeant Larry Sim, and Chaplin Arthur Williams.

Marian Anderson

Marian Anderson was the most celebrated singer in the twentieth century. She was the first Negro to perform at the White House and the first Negro to sing with New York's Metropolitan Opera. Anderson helped launch the civil rights movement and helped to improve race relations in the United States when she sang My Country 'Tis of Thee on the steps of the Lincoln Memorial on April 9, 1939, because the Daughters of the American Revolution refused to let a Negro sing in Constitution Hall; only whites could sing on their stage. Executive Secretary of the NAACP Walter White came up with the idea for Anderson to sing outdoors at the Lincoln Memorial National Monument because the audience was too large to fit into any other auditorium in the city. *I could not run away from this situation. If I had anything to offer, I would have to do so now.*

During World War II, Marian Anderson entertained soldiers in hospitals and bases. In September 1942, the Daughters of the American Revolution invited Anderson to perform for a series of benefit concerts of the Army Emergency Relief Fund. Anderson agreed to perform only if there were no segregation of Negroes at the concert and if the recital would set a precedent allowing her use of the hall in the future. Initially, DAR declined Anderson's terms, but the two were able to reach a compromise agreement. On January 7, 1943, she sang to an integrated audience at Constitution Hall as part of a benefit for the Red Cross with no commitments about future engagements or any change in the openly racist booking policy. The hall was filled to capacity, filling 3,844 seats with distinguished guests and other dignitaries, including the President of the United States, Franklin D. Roosevelt, Mrs. Roosevelt, House and cabinet members, the Chinese Ambassador, and Supreme Court Justices Hugo Black and William O. Douglas. The momentous recital raised $6,500 for the United China Relief.

On April 9, 1939, Marian Anderson performed for 75,000 people on the steps of the Lincoln Memorial after being denied use of a DC Hall over segregation rules.

MARIAN ANDERSON

★ ★ **EASTER SUNDAY 1939** ★ ★

FREE CONCERT AT NOON! ! !

LINCOLN MEMORIAL - WASHINGTON, D. C.

Marian Anderson sing at the Lincoln Memorial, Washington, DC 1939

Eleanor Roosevelt presenting the NAACP 1939 Spingarn Medal to Marian Anderson. In 1939, Anderson delivered Nobody Knows the Trouble I've Seen and America with heart breaking pathos at her concert on the steps of the Lincoln Memorial.

Marian Anderson, world's greatest contralto, April 2, 1945

Marian Anderson and United States Naval officials, November 7, 1942

Marian Anderson singing at the United States Naval Training Center, Great Lakes, Illinois, June 30, 1944

Marian Anderson and Robert Gray taking an oath at Constitution Hall during a swearing-in ceremony, Washington, DC, 1960

Marian Anderson receiving the Liberian Order of African Redemption

IN THIS TEMPLE
AS IN THE HEARTS OF THE PEOPLE
FOR WHOM HE SAVED THE UNION
THE MEMORY OF ABRAHAM LINCOLN
IS ENSHRINED FOREVER

MARIAN ANDERSON
AT FT. LOGAN.
FEB. 23, 1945
BY ARRANGEMENT
WITH
HAZEL M. OBERFELDER

Marian Anderson sings the Star Spangled Banner

Marian Anderson christens SS (Sailing Ship) Booker T. Washington on September 29, 1942 at the California Shipbuilding Corporation's Wilmington yards.

Marian Anderson christens SS Booker T. Washington

Marian Anderson, Mary McLeod Bethune, and other dignitaries at the launching of the SS Booker T. Washington on September 29, 1942 at the California Shipbuilding Corporation's Wilmington yards. The SS Booker T. Washington was the first Liberty Ship named in honor of a Negro.

Mary McLeod Bethune, Marian Anderson, and Dr, William J. Thompkins, Recorder of Deeds, Washington, DC congratulates workmen who helped construct the SS Booker T. Washington.

Marian Anderson, Mary McLeod Bethune, and defense workers at the launching of the SS Booker T. Washington on September 29, 1942 at the California Shipbuilding Corporation's Wilmington yards.

Elaine Mulzac, daughter of Captain Hugh Mulzac, skipper of the SS Booker T. Washington, on September 29, 1942, talks to two workmen who helped construct the first Liberty Ship named in honor of a Negro.

Negro Crew of the SS Booker T. Washington, Lastic, Young, Hlubk, Smith, Captain Hugh Mulzac, Fokes, Kruley, Rutland, and Larson, after her maiden voyage to England, February 8, 1943.

Marian Anderson, world's greatest contralto, entertains a group of veterans and WACs on stage at the San Antonio Municipal Auditorium in San Antonio, Texas, April 11, 1945

Joe Louis Barrow, *the Brown Bomber*

Joe Louis Barrow, *the Brown Bomber,* was the World Heavyweight Boxing Champion from 1937 through 1949. In 1942, he fought two charity bouts. The first bout was against Buddy Baer on January 9 for the Navy Relief Society, raising $47,000. However, he enlisted in the army on January 10, 1942, and Louis was a soldier when he fought the second bout on March 23 against Abe Simon, raising $36,000 for the Army Relief Fund.

During his enlistment, Louis toured military facilities throughout the United States and Europe putting on 96 exhibitions bouts. On August 30, 1943, Louis put on an exhibition at Fort Devens and Camp Edwards. At Camp Edwards, his opponent was First Sergeant George Nicholson. Before being discharged in 1945, he achieved the rank of Technical Sergeant First Class and was awarded the Legion of Merit.

March 24, 1942, Joe Louis training for his upcoming fight in Madison Square Garden

Joe Louis and George Nicholson Training at Fort Dix for his 21st title defense

Joe Louis is going through the proper motions during the Command Inspection Arms, Fort Dix, New Jersey, 1942.

Private Joe Louis, Heavy Weight Champion, arrives at Fort Dix, New Jersey, to train to defend his title against Abe Simon at Madison Square Garden on April 27, 1942, for the benefit of the Army Emergency Fund.

Joe Louis shaking Colonel William A. Smith's hand during hospital tour at Fort Devens

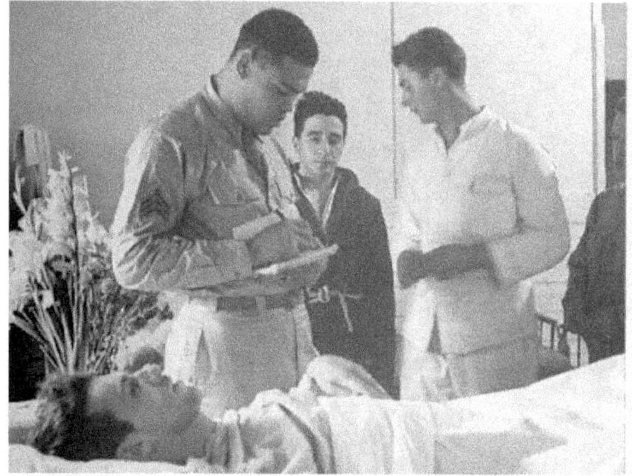

Joe Louis signing autographs during hospital tour at Fort Devens

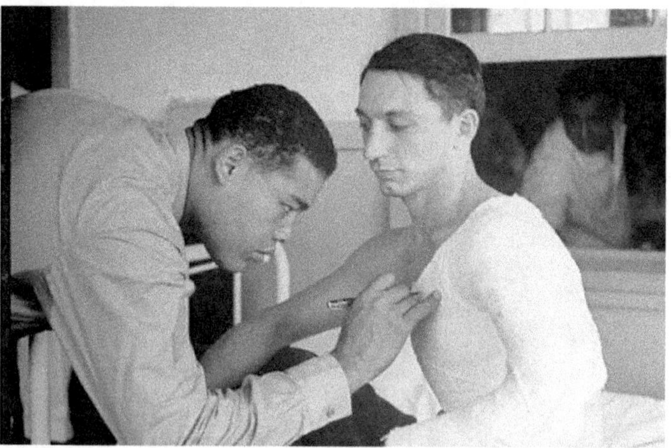

Joe Louis autographing patient's cast during hospital tour at Fort Devens

Boxers James Edgar, Jackie Fields, Joe Louis, and Sugar Ray Robinson at Veteran's Hospital, September 1943

Joe Louis signing autographs during tour of Fort Devens

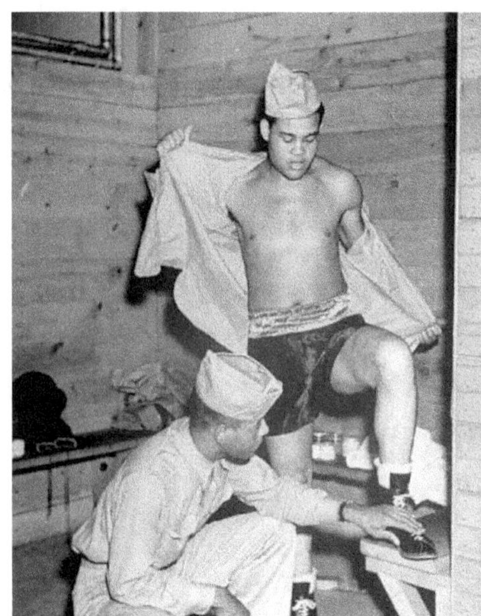

Joe Louis preparing for an exhibition bout during a tour at Fort Devens

Joe Louis and other soldiers with veterans in bathrobes in the yard of the Veteran's Hospital, Butler, Pennsylvania, September 1943.

Joe Louis reviewing WAC Trainees during a tour of Fort Devens

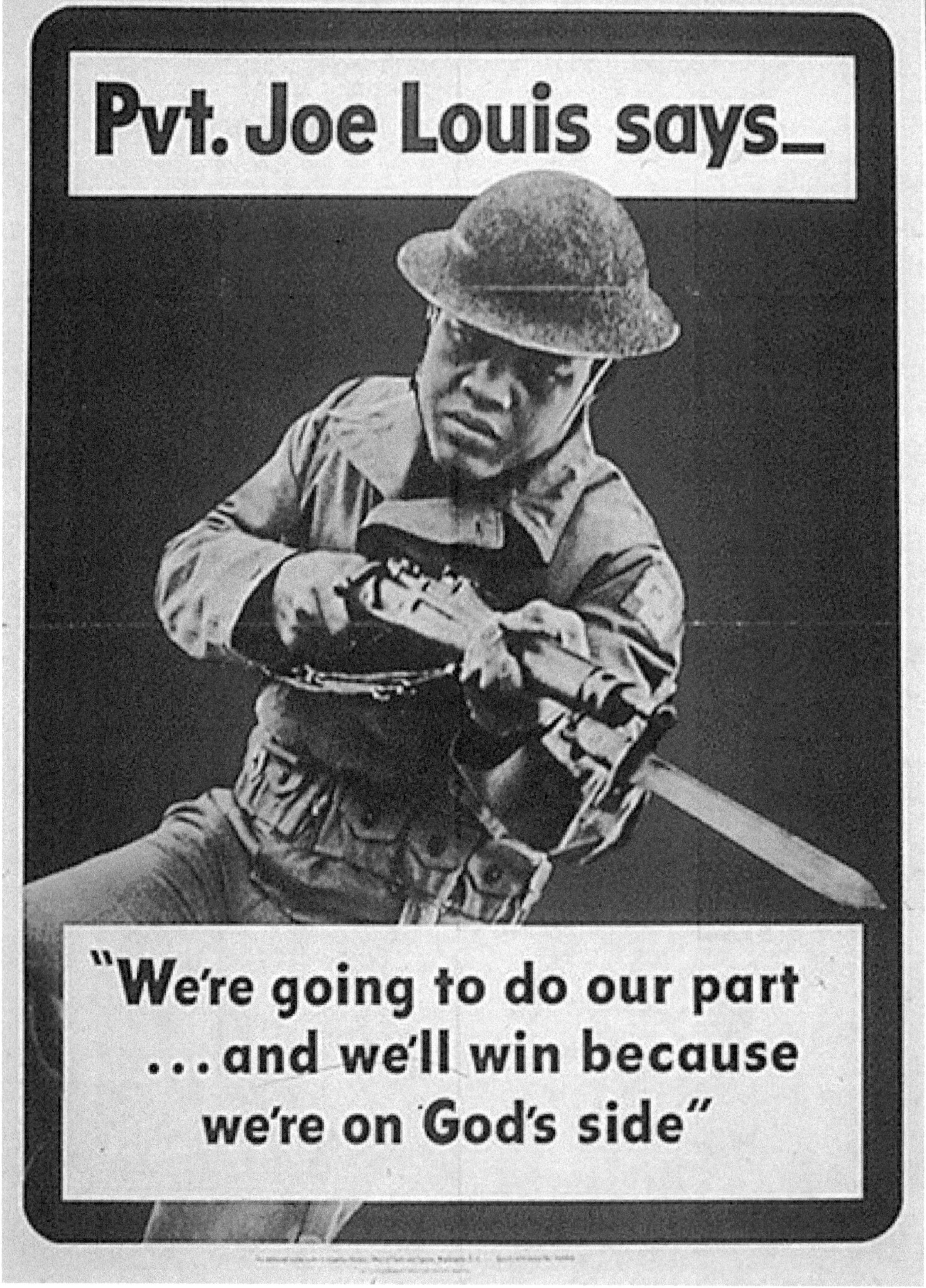

Pvt. Joe Louis says_

"We're going to do our part ...and we'll win because we're on God's side"

Sergeant Joe Louis, Truman K. Gibson, Jr. and Colonel Stanley J. Grogan discussing plans for boxing shows for American soldier's world tour, July 11, 1943.

World Heavy Weight Champion, Joe Louis Barrow and fellow Sergeant George Nicholson, opponent, talking before exhibition, London, April 11, 1944.

London April 11, 1944

World Heavy Weight Champion, Joe Louis Barrow and fellow Sergeant George Nicholson, opponent, talking before exhibition, London, April 11, 1944.

Joe Louis fighting in an exhibition in London, 1944

Joe Louis heading toward neutral corner in fight at Madison Square Garden against Clarence Red Burman with Referee Frank Fullam.

Tech Sergeant Joe Louis stops to talk with two Eskimo boys with their huskie dog during a tour of the USAAF in the Central Canada Command at Southampton Island, Canada

Sergeant Joe Louis and General Davis, the first Negro General in the United States Army

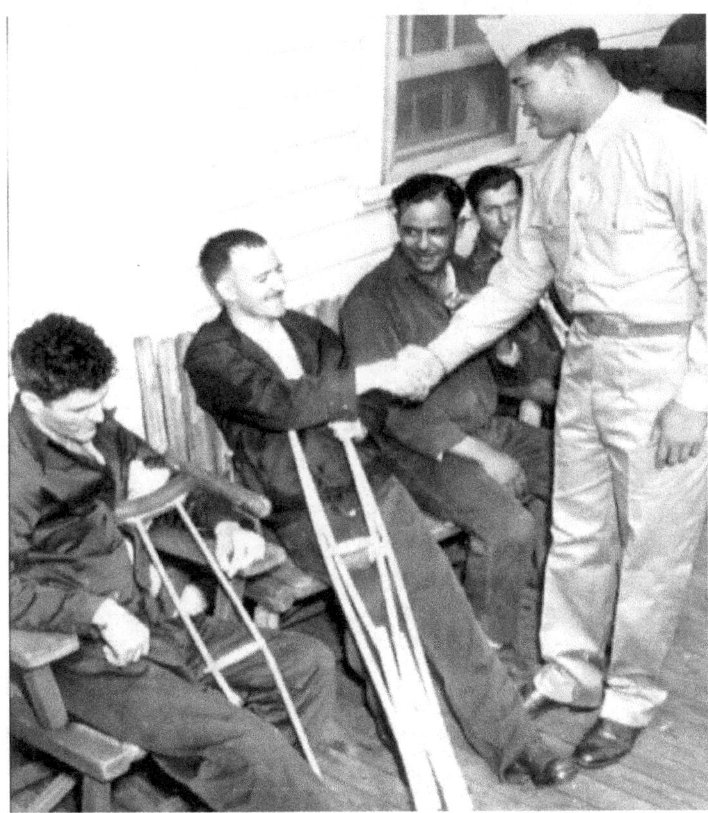

Sergeant Joe Louis greeting veterans of war

Sergeant Joe Louis and cast of The Well Dressed Man in Harlem featured in This is the Army

Joe Louis entering fighter cockpit

gettyimages
Metronome

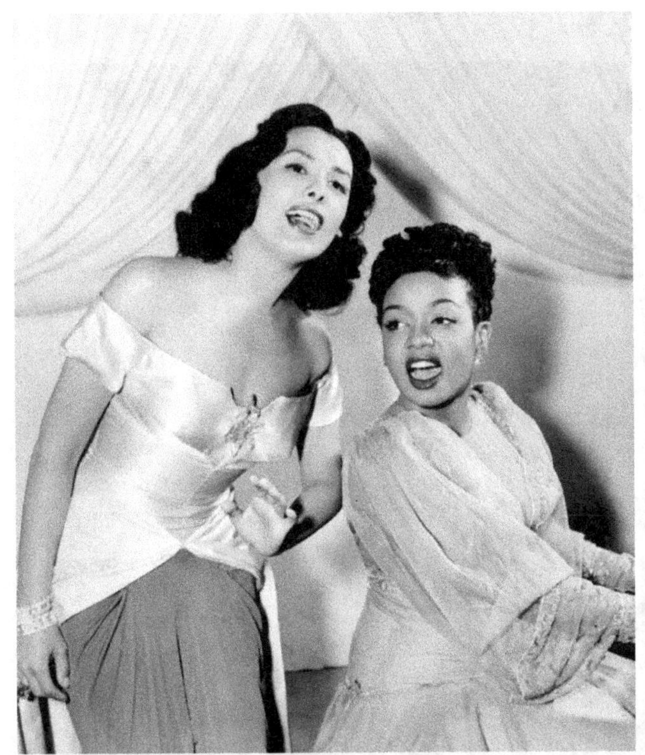

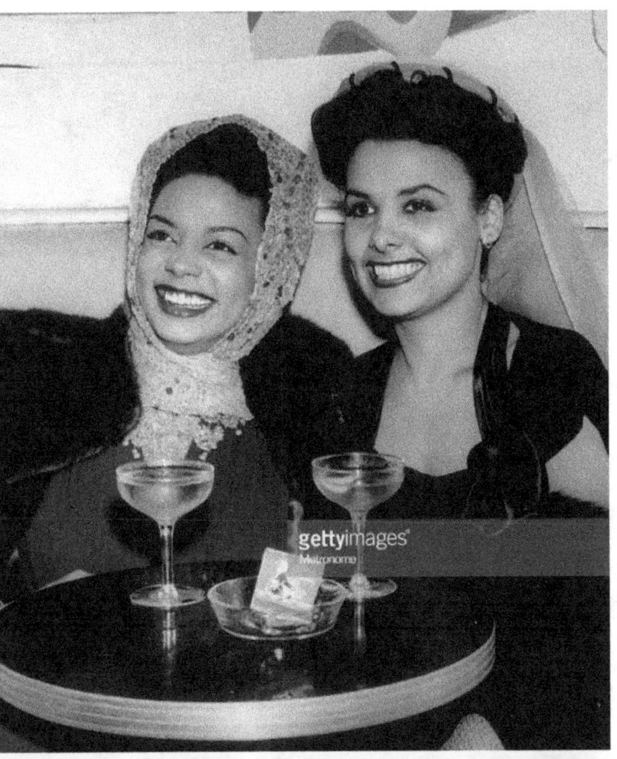

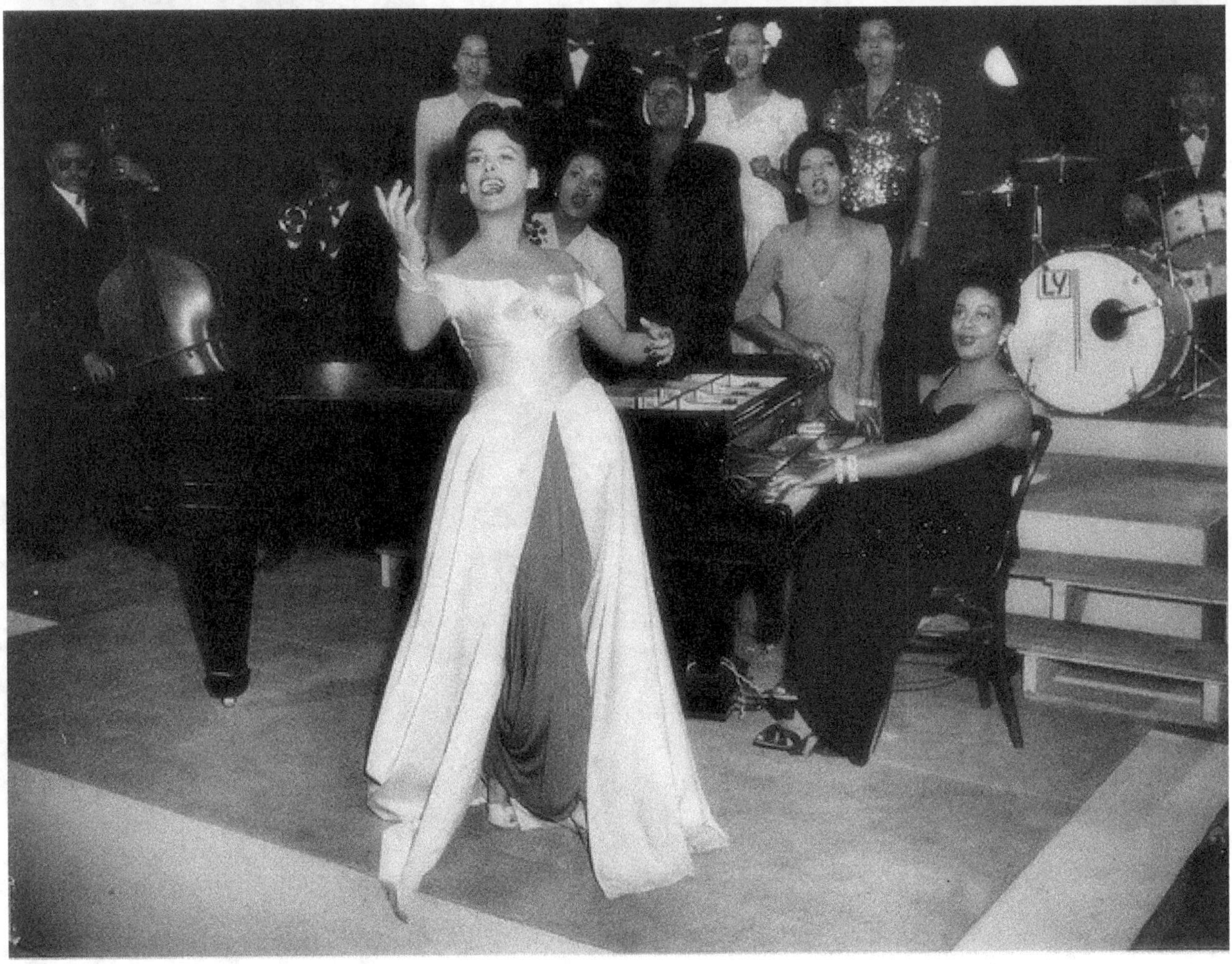

Hazel Scott

Trinidadian born jazz and classical pianist, actress, and singer, Hazel Dorothy Scott was the first Afro Caribbean woman to star in her own nationally syndicated television show in the United States. The Hazel Show premiered on the DuMont Television Network on July 3, 1950. Hazel Scott contributed to the war effort by performing for U.S. troops, both at home and abroad. She participated in USO shows and benefit concerts, boosting morale and raising funds for war-related causes. Her performances were especially significant because she insisted on playing for integrated audiences, refusing to entertain segregated crowds—a bold stance for the time.

In 1942, President Roosevelt ordered a nationwide gas rationing. Lena Horne in an ad showing all Americans how they can help in the war effort by conserving fuel.

The Legendary Lena Horne

The Legendary Lena Horne at the age of 25 was the first Negro performer to sign a long-term contract with a major Hollywood Studio, Metro Goldwyn. Lena Horne was also the first Negro performer to tour with an all-white band.

During World War II, she refused to perform for segregated audiences and on one occasion while performing at Fort Reilly, Kansas, she moved to the back of the room where Negro soldiers were forced to sit in the back of the hall behind German prisoners of War. She left the stage immediately and filed a complaint with the NAACP about the occurrence. MGM Studios pulled her from the tour. As a result, Lena continued her tour to entertain Negro soldiers self-financing her travels.

Harry Torczyner, Chief of the Office of the War Information Belgian Desk interviews Lena Horne on the Voice of America Program

Lena Horne visiting the Tuskegee Airmen

The Jungle Band, the Army's hottest Negro Musicians, dressed in dappled jungle suits, listening to Lena Horne sing a number with hot pianist *Sinky* Hendricks. The band members were members of the 299th Army Ground Force Band; however, before the war members played with top-flight bands including Cab Calloway and Count Basie.

Lena Horne singing to soldiers at the Hollywood Canteen.

Lena Horne with friends and Tuskegee Airmen

Lena Horne singing to soldiers at the Hollywood Canteen.

Lena talking to soldier and USO worker

Lena Horne visiting and signing autographs for soldiers

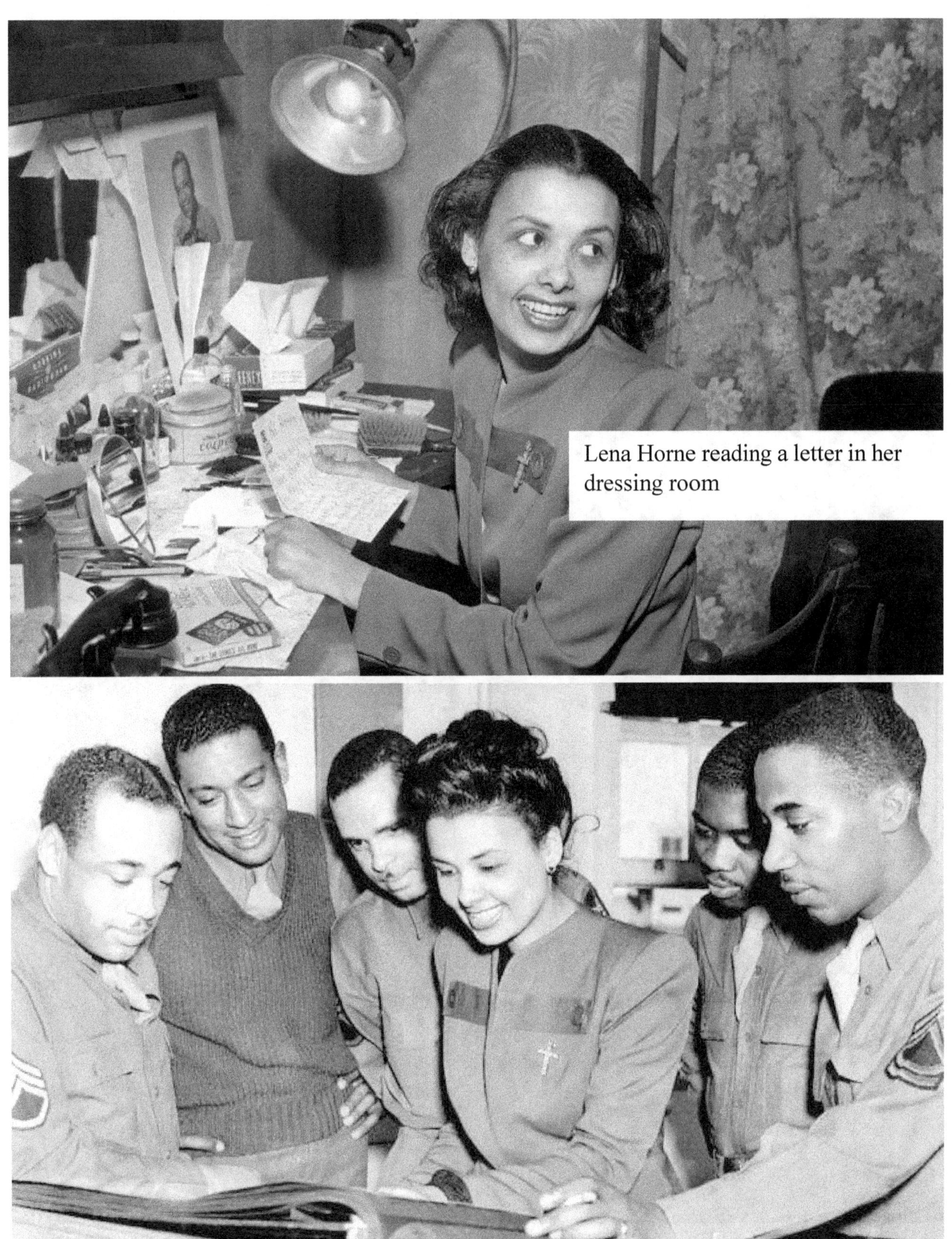

Lena Horne reading a letter in her dressing room

Lena Horne visiting and signing autographs for army soldiers

Tuskegee Airmen and Brigadier General Noel Parrish with Lena Horne at a banquet at Tuskegee Institute

WAC reading paper with Lena Horne November 23, 1944

Lena Horne and General Davis, the first Negro General in the United States Army

SS George Washington Carver, Liberty Ship

Lena Horne addressing the audience at a war bond rally before the christening of the second liberty ship named in honor of a Negro, the SS George Washington Carver, Liberty Ship in Henry J. Kaiser Shipyard No. 1, Richmond, California on May 7, 1943.

Lena Horne christening the second liberty ship named in honor of a Negro, the SS George Washington Carver, Liberty Ship in Henry J. Kaiser Shipyard No. 1, Richmond, California, on May 7, 1943. The SS George Washington Liberty Ship was built by skilled Negro workers. 7,000 Negroes worked in four Kaiser Shipyards. Approximately 1,000 of the shipyard's skilled workers were women.

Lena Horne about to place a kiss on the cheek of Montrose Carrol, a chipper who worked on the Liberty Ship

Lena Horne signing autographs for shipyard workers who helped to build the SS George Washington Liberty Ship

SS Robert S. Abbott Liberty Ship

SS Robert S. Abbott Liberty Ship named in honor Chicago Defender Newspaper founder, Robert S. Abbott.

John H. Sengstacke, publisher of the Chicago Defender and nephew of Robert S. Abbott at Permanente Metals Corporation Shipyard Number 2, Richmond, California, on April 13, 1944

Chicago Defender publisher John H. Sengstacke and wife Myrtle with family and friends during festivities celebrating the launch of the Liberty Ship SS Robert S. Abbott.

Lulu Mae Hamel presenting a bouquet of flowers to Myrtle Sengstacke wife of Chicago Defender publisher John H. Sengstacke

Myrtle Sengstacke wife of Chicago Defender publisher John H. Sengstacke

Myrtle Sengstacke with friends and family at Permanente Metals Corporation Shipyard Number 2, Richmond, California, on April 13, 1944.

John H. Sengstacke, publisher of the Chicago Defender and nephew of Robert S. Abbott and his wife Myrtle and members of the launch party for the Liberty Ship SS Robert S. Abbott at Permanente Metals Corporation Shipyard Number 2, Richmond, California, on April 13, 1944

Members of the launch party for the Liberty Ship SS Robert S. Abbott, John H. Sengstake, Myrtle Sengstacke who sponsored the ship holding the launch bottle ready, Captain Euclid Louis Taylor, counsel for the Chicago Defender, unidentified woman, Ms Lulu Mae Hamel who sold eighty thousand dollars' worth of War Bonds, and rest are unidentified.

John H. Murphy, Sr.

Captain Godfrey standing with four relatives of John H. Murphy, Sr. (from left to right Mr. and Mrs. George B. Murphy, Sr., son and daughter-in-law; Mrs. John Murphy; and Miss Frances Murphy, daughter) at the launching of the Liberty Ship John H. Murphy, Sr. at the Bethlehem Fairfield Shipyard.

SS Edward A. Savoy

Descendants of the late Edward A. Savoy at the launch of the Liberty Ship SS Edward A. Savoy Bethlehem Fairfield Shipyard

Mrs. Edith Savoy Morgan, daughter of the late Edward A. Savoy, christens the Liberty Ship SS Edward A. Savoy, Bethlehem airfield Shipyard

SS Frederick Douglass

Frederick Douglass III, grandson of the noted Abolitionist, addressing the workers and congratulating the crew of the SS Frederick Douglass on the day of its launching.

SS Frederick Douglass Captain and Crew

Anne Wiggens Brown, Baltimore born concert singer, christened SS Frederick Douglass at the Bethlehem-Fairchild Shipyards in Baltimore, Maryland, on May 22, 1943. The SS Frederick Douglass was the third Liberty Ship named for an outstanding Negro.

Liberty Ship SS Harriett Tubman

The Liberty Ship SS Harriett Tubman christening ceremony South Portland, Maine, June 3, 1944.

Mrs. E.S. Northup, grandniece of Harriett Tubman, christening the Liberty Ship SS Harriett Tubman, South Portland, Maine, June 3, 1944.

Miss Hilda Proctor of Yonkers, New York, Mrs. Mary Cornish of Chester, Pennsylvania, Mrs. E.S. Northup, grandniece of Harriet Tubman of Philadelphia, and Mrs. Marylin of Philadelphia at the launching ceremony, South Portland, Maine, June 3, 1944.

SS Hall Young

Beulah Whittington, ship worker, receiving a bouquet of American Beauty roses from Frank Stearns of Richmond Shipyard No. 2 as Katie Lewis, matron of honor, looks on during the ship launching of the SS Hall Young at Richmond Shipyard No. 2.

US Navy LSM Vessel No. 325

US Navy Landing Ship Medium Vessel No. 325 launching party. Mrs. Lula Martin, Chicago, Illinois sponsor, August 25, 1944

SS John Hope

Mr. Walter Gordon, daughter Betty Gordon, and Elizabeth Gordon at the launching of the SS John Hope.

SS Robert L. Vann

Mrs. Jessie Matthews Vann, Robert L. Vann's widow standing between SS Robert L. Vann Deck Engineer Walter E. Harris, Jr. and Warrant Officer William E. Simmons in the Lafayette Hotel for the liberty ship's christening ceremony, Portland, Maine, on October 10, 1943.

Pier for the christening of the SS Robert L. Vann

Toki Schalk Johnson, two unknown women, Mable Page Johnson, Daisy Lampkin, Jesse Vann, Blanche Morris, and Harriet Lewis standing in front of stone building for christening ceremony of the SS Robert L. Vann, Portland, Maine, October 10, 1943.

Group in front of World War II propaganda posters

Lillian Von Schalk, Mrs. Harris, Norman Harris, Toki Schalk Johnson, and Lorena Cuzzena

Andrew Sides, P.L. Prattis, Jessie Vann holding large bouquet of flowers, and Mable Page surrounded by group

Mrs. Tabor, Edward O. Tabor, and Jessie Vann standing in hallway of the Lafayette Hotel for christening ceremony

Homer S. Brown, Ira F. Lewis, Thomas E. Kilgallen, Ward Freeman, Edward O. Tabor, and

Mrs. Jessie Matthews Vann, Robert L. Vann's widow standing between SS Robert L. Vann Deck Engineer Walter E. Harris, Jr. and Warrant Officer William E. Simmons in the Lafayette Hotel for the liberty ship's christening ceremony, Portland, Maine, on October 10, 1943.

Deck Engineer Walter E. Harris, Jr. and Warrant Officer William E. Simmons

SS Robert L. Vann

Mrs. Ira F. Lewis, wife of the president of the Pittsburgh Courier Publishing Company, presents a photo of the late Robert L. Vann

Cake with picture of the Liberty Ship SS Robert L. Vann on table, decorated with leaves and basket of flowers in interior

Jessie Vann holding up silver dish from the New England Shipbuilding Corporation and standing between Bill Nunn, Sr. and Andrew Sides surrounded by group including Chester Churchill, William McCaffrey, Andrew Red Pettis, Elnar Edwards, and Timothy Crean

Andrew Sides, P.L. Prattis, Jessie Vann, holding a large bouquet of flowers, and Mable Page, surrounded by a group

Chester L. Washington, Jr., Harriet Lewis, Daisy E. Lampkin, Ira F. Lewis, Jessie Vann holding a large bouquet of flowers, Mable Page Johnson, P.L. Prattis, and George Schuyler

Mrs. Jessie Matthews Vann christening Liberty Ship SS Robert L. Vann. With Mable Page Johnson holding a bouquet of flowers, Portland, Maine, October 10, 1943.

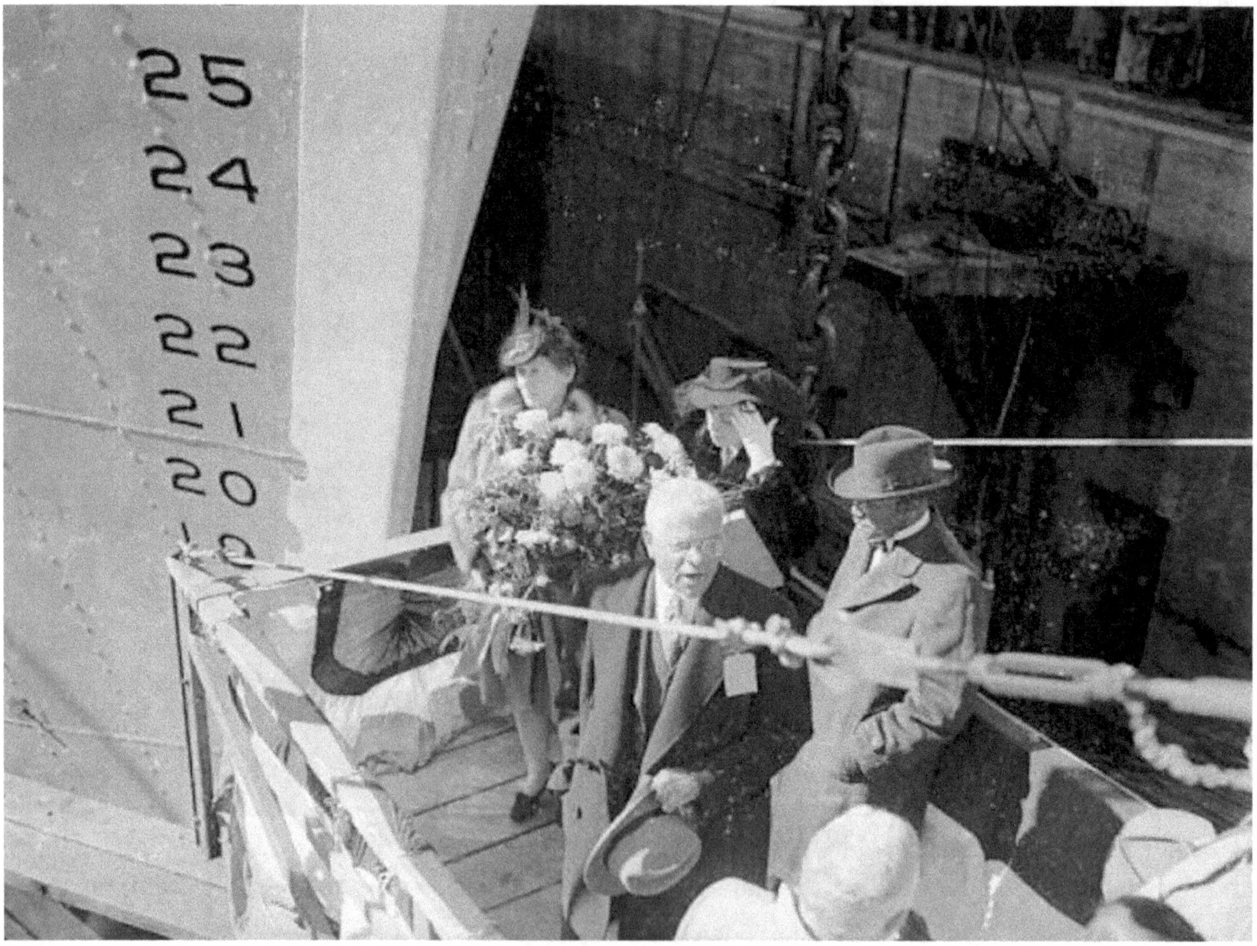

Mrs. Jessie Matthews Vann holding a bouquet of flowers and flanked by CC Spaulding, president of the North Carolina Mutual Life Insurance and Dr. Emmett J. Scott of the Sun Shipbuilding Company at the launch of the SS Robert L. Vann

Their Story Lives

In reflecting upon the lives, service, and contributions of the WAVES, SPARS, and the remarkable Black Americans who shaped our nation during World War II, we are reminded that history is not only recorded in battles won or ships launched, but in the courage of individuals who refused to be defined by limitation. Their stories of determination, brilliance, patriotism, resilience, and sacrifice continue to echo across generations.

These women and men stepped forward during a time when the world was at war, and America was struggling with its own divisions. They served, performed, built, healed, inspired, and led, not only for victory abroad but for dignity and equality at home. Each photograph, each caption, and each biography contained in these pages reinforces one truth: progress is built by those who dare to break barriers.

By preserving their legacies, we ensure that their contributions are neither forgotten nor minimized. We acknowledge their challenges, celebrate their triumphs, and honor the paths they forged, paths that continue to guide us toward a more just and inclusive future.

May this collection serve not only as a record of the past, but as an invitation to future generations to learn, question, aspire, and persevere. The stories within these pages remind us that heroism takes many forms and that even in the most turbulent times, ordinary people can achieve extraordinary things.

Let their legacy continue to inspire us to serve with courage, lead with compassion, and stand, always, on the side of justice.

References

Crawford, A. (1988). *Women in the U.S. military: An annotated bibliography*. Garland Publishing.

Joyner Library Special Collections. (2025). *SPARs: The women who served in the U.S. Coast Guard during World War II*. East Carolina University.

Miller, R. (1979). *The Navy's WAVES: Women in the Navy in World War II*. Naval Institute Press.

Mundell, E. H. (1949). *The United States Coast Guard in World War II*. U.S. Government Printing Office.

Naval History & Heritage Command. (1948). *United States Naval Reserve in World War II*. U.S. Navy Department.

Navy Bureau of Personnel. (1944). *WAVES training manual*. U.S. Government Printing Office.

Navy Department. (1945). *The Negro in the Navy*. U.S. Government Printing Office.

Navy Recruiting Station. (1943). *Facts about the WAVES and SPARS*. U.S. Government Printing Office.

Parker, M. (1990). *SPARS: The Women's Reserve of the U.S. Coast Guard in World War II*. Naval Institute Press.

Scrivener, L. (1999). *U.S. military women in World War II: The SPAR, WAC, WAVES, WASP, and Women Marines in U.S. government publications*. Elsevier.

Sherman, C. (1946). *The Coast Guard at War: Women's Reserve*. U.S. Government Printing Office.

Stratton, D. C. (1946). *The lady and the Coast Guard*. U.S. Coast Guard Press.

Treadwell, M. E. (1954). *The Women's Army Corps*. U.S. Army Center of Military History.

Truman, H. S. (1948). *Executive Order 9981: Desegregation of the Armed Forces*. U.S. Government Printing Office.

U.S. Coast Guard. (n.d.). *SPARS: The Coast Guard & the Women's Reserve in World War II*. U.S. Department of Homeland Security.

U.S. Coast Guard. (n.d.). *Women in the Coast Guard: A historical overview*. U.S. Department of Homeland Security.

U.S. Maritime Commission. (1942–1945). *Ship launching records and christening logs*. U.S. Government Printing Office.

U.S. Maritime Commission. (1947). *Liberty ships: The history of the emergency shipbuilding program*. U.S. Government Printing Office.

U.S. War Department. (1942–1945). *Special Services Division records: Morale, recreation, and athletic programs*. U.S. Government Printing Office.

www.ingramcontent.com/pod-product-compliance
Lightning Source LLC
LaVergne TN
LVHW080334110826
845155LV00027B/242
9781953824189